Picture the Past
Life on the Underground Railroad

Sally Senzell Isaacs

Heinemann Library
Chicago, Illinois

© 2002 Reed Educational & Professional Publishing
Published by Heinemann Library,
an imprint of Reed Educational & Professional Publishing,
Chicago, IL
Customer Service 888-454-2279
Visit our website at www.heinemannlibrary.com

Produced for Heinemann Library by
    Bender Richardson White.
Editor: Lionel Bender
Designer and Media Conversion: Ben White
Picture Researcher: Cathy Stastny
Production Controller: Kim Richardson

06 05 04 03 02
10 9 8 7 6 5 4 3 2 1

Printed in Hong Kong

Library of Congress Cataloging-in-Publication Data.
Isaacs, Sally Senzell, 1950-
    Life on the Underground Railroad / Sally Senzell Isaacs.
        p. cm. -- (Picture the past)
    Includes bibliographical references (p.) and index.
        ISBN 1-58810-253-X (hb. bdg.) ISBN 1-58810-418-4
(pbk. bdg.)
    1. Underground railroad--Juvenile literature.
2. Fugitive slaves--United States--Social conditions--
Juvenile literature. (1.Underground railroad. 2. Fugitive
slaves.) I. Title.
    E450 .I8 2001
    973.7'15--dc21
                                    2001000499

Special thanks to Mike Carpenter at Heinemann Library
for editorial and design guidance and direction.

Acknowledgments
The producers and publishers are grateful to the follow-
ing for permission to reproduce copyright material:
The Bridgeman Art Library/Private Collection, page 28.
Corbis Images: Bettman Archive, page 20; Bettman
Archive/Range, page 29; Hulton-Deutsch Collection,
page 26. Library of Congress: pages 16 and 30. North
Wind Pictures: pages 9, 15, 17, 22, and 24. Peter
Newark's American Pictures: pages 3, 7, 8, 10, 11, 13, 14,
and 25.
Cover photograph: Peter Newarks's American Pictures.

Every effort has been made to contact copyright hold-
ers of any material reproduced in this book. Omissions
will be rectified in subsequent printings if notice is given
to the publisher.

Illustrations by Mark Bergin, pages 6, 26–27; John James,
pages 18, 19, 23; Gerald Wood, page 12.
Map by Stefan Chabluk.
Cover make-up: Mike Pilley, Radius.

Note to the Reader
Some words are shown in bold, **like this**.
You can find out what they mean by
looking in the glossary.

ABOUT THIS BOOK

This book tells about the people
who ran away from slavery in the
southern United States from 1830
to 1860. It also tells about the
people who helped slaves escape to
freedom. Some information about
the "Underground Railroad" was
written down by the people who
helped the slaves. By law, most
slaves could not learn to write.
So their viewpoints were told in
stories and songs passed down from
grandparents to children. We have
illustrated the book with paintings,
drawings, and photographs of the
time. We also include artists' ideas
of how things looked in the days of
the Underground Railroad.

The Author
Sally Senzell Isaacs is a professional writer
and editor of nonfiction books for children.
She graduated from Indiana University,
earning a B.S. degree in Education with
majors in American History and Sociology.
For some years, she was the Editorial
Director of Reader's Digest Educational
Division. Sally Senzell Isaacs lives in New
Jersey with her husband and two children.

CONTENTS

Underground Railroad

Before 1860, there were about four million slaves in the United States. A slave was a person who was owned by another person. Slaves worked without pay. Sometimes owners made slaves work even when they were sick or hurt. From 1830 to 1860, thousands of slaves ran away from their owners. They ran from hiding place to hiding place until they reached cities in the **North** where slavery was not allowed. These hiding places and the people who helped the slaves were called the Underground Railroad.

Look for these
The illustrations of a runaway boy and girl show you the subject of each double-page story in the book.

The illustrations of slave chains put on slaves highlight boxes with facts and figures about life on the Underground Railroad.

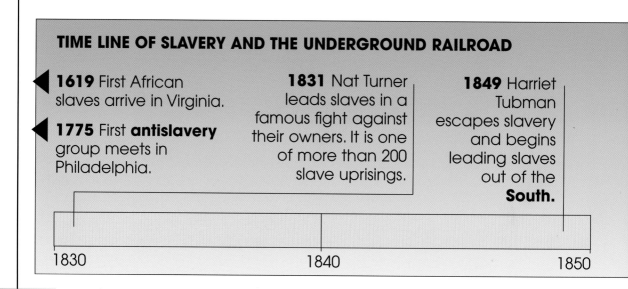

TIME LINE OF SLAVERY AND THE UNDERGROUND RAILROAD

1619 First African slaves arrive in Virginia.

1775 First **antislavery** group meets in Philadelphia.

1831 Nat Turner leads slaves in a famous fight against their owners. It is one of more than 200 slave uprisings.

1849 Harriet Tubman escapes slavery and begins leading slaves out of the **South.**

1830   1840   1850

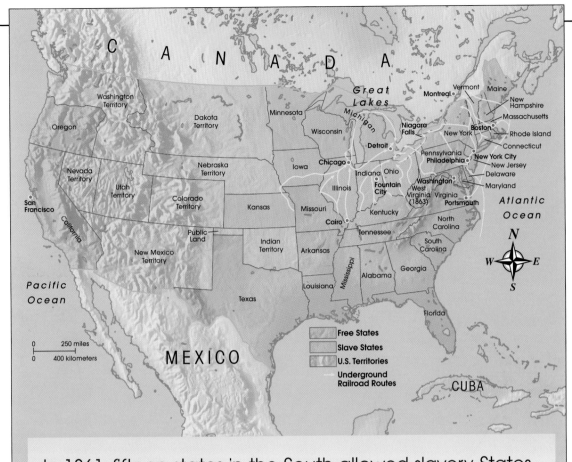

In 1861, fifteen states in the South allowed slavery. States in the North did not allow it. Runaway slaves had to sneak out of the South and go to a northern state or to Canada.

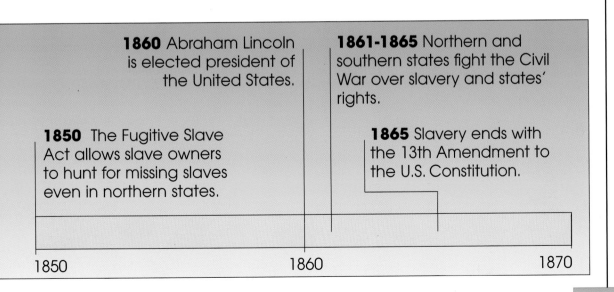

1850 The Fugitive Slave Act allows slave owners to hunt for missing slaves even in northern states.

1860 Abraham Lincoln is elected president of the United States.

1861-1865 Northern and southern states fight the Civil War over slavery and states' rights.

1865 Slavery ends with the 13th Amendment to the U.S. Constitution.

1850   1860   1870

Slaves

The Africans were rounded up and crowded onto ships. Many Africans got sick and died on the ships. Some broke their iron chains and fought to get free.

From 1619 to 1808, thousands of Africans came to America. They did not choose to come. They had been living in African villages with their families and friends. Suddenly, strangers grabbed them, locked their hands in chains, and marched them to waiting ships.

The ships took the Africans to America. Many were sold to **plantation** owners in the southern states. The Africans became slaves for the owners. They would work hard, with no pay and no freedom to leave. When the Africans had children, they would belong to the owners, too.

The Plantation

Most slaves worked on **plantations.** A plantation is a large farm that mostly grows one **crop,** such as cotton. Growing and selling cotton made some plantation owners wealthy. But they needed many workers to plant, pick, and pack the crops. They could not become rich without slaves to do the work.

FORBIDDEN MEETINGS

Owners were scared that the slaves might plan to run away. There were laws against slaves holding meetings, except at church on Sunday. Even then, a white **preacher** had to be there.

Slaves worked from sunrise to sunset. There was little time to rest. Some owners beat their slaves for not working hard enough.

Slaves lived in small cabins by the fields. They returned to their cabins after a long day's work. They cooked the little bit of food that the owners gave them. They often sang songs and told stories to forget their troubles. Sometimes they whispered about plans to run away.

A slave girl sits by the fireplace in her cabin. Often ten people shared one small cabin. The floors were made of wood. People cooked at the fireplace.

The Escape

Many people wanted to help slaves escape to the northern states where there was no slavery. These people gave the slaves food, clothes, and hiding places. These people called themselves the Underground Railroad. They used the word "underground" because slaves were hidden in secret places. They were like a "railroad" because they planned special **routes** to follow and places to stop.

Some experts say around 5,000 slaves escaped from **plantations** between 1830 and 1860. Others say 100,000 slaves escaped.

RAILROAD NAMES

Slaves used code words to talk about their escape:
• **Station**—a safe house for hiding
• **Station master**—person who owned a safe house
• **Conductor**—someone who led the slaves from station to station
• **Passengers**—runaway slaves

Some owners locked bells around their slaves. This made it easier to find the slaves if they ran away.

Slaves found out about the Underground Railroad in many ways. Sometimes a runaway slave secretly returned to the plantation to guide others away. Or a white person told a slave about a friend's house that was a safe hiding place. Always, people spoke in codes and secret messages.

Secret Messages

Slaves received secret messages from people who were making plans to escape. Sometimes the plantation's **blacksmith** pounded out a code with his hammer. He told the slaves when to leave.

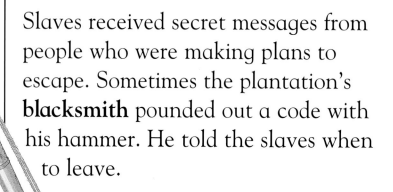

When a boat arrived in the **South,** many slaves came aboard to load it. Sometimes slaves received secret messages from free African Americans who worked on the ship.

ESCAPE SONG

These are the words to the song *Follow the Drinking Gourd.*

*"When the sun comes back and the first quail calls, follow the Drinking Gourd.
For the old man is waiting for to carry you to freedom, if you follow the Drinking Gourd."*

These words tell the slaves to leave when the quails (birds) come to the South for the winter. An old man, named Peg Leg Joe, will meet the slaves and lead them north.

*"The river bank makes a very good road. The dead trees show you the way.
Left foot, peg foot, traveling on. Follow the Drinking Gourd."*

The slaves should go north, following the shore of the Tombighee River. Joe's foot print and peg print will mark a trail.

Slaves often heard songs that told them about a route. One song was called *Follow the Drinking Gourd.* The Drinking Gourd was another name for the pattern of stars in the Little Dipper. The North Star shines at the top of the Drinking Gourd. By walking toward the North Star, the slaves would head in the direction of the **free states.**

As slaves danced, their steps sometimes told secret messages about running away.

Into the Night

When slaves ran away, they took a small bit of food and the clothes they were wearing. They crept out at night while their owners slept. Once an owner noticed slaves missing, he took off after them. He also nailed posters in all the towns, describing the slaves and offering a reward. If slaves were caught, they were punished.

Slave owners used dogs to find runaway slaves. The dogs smelled the slaves' clothes and blankets and followed the **scent.**

ON THE TRAIL

Many slave owners used dogs called **bloodhounds.** This kind of dog has a very good sense of smell. Today, bloodhounds are still used for hunting animals and finding missing people.

Slaves ran at night and hid during the day. Some ran to Florida, which was not part of the United States until 1845. They lived among the Seminole **Native Americans.** Most slaves headed north where there was no slavery. They went to the **free states** and to Canada.

Runaway slaves crossed swamps, rivers, forests, and fields. There were many different **routes** to the **North.**

Helpers

Many people believed that slavery was wrong. Thousands of them helped slaves reach freedom. Many sewed clothing and collected medicine and food. Some were "station masters." They allowed slaves to hide in their attics and basements. Others were "conductors." They secretly carried the slaves in their wagons and boats.

HELPFUL SOUNDS

Slaves knew that some "conductors" made sound signals. One family stood by a river and made bird calls to guide the slaves to shore.

These runaway slaves arrived in boats. "Conductors" hid them in wagons and drove them farther north. In southern states, people who were caught helping slaves were punished.

Harriet Tubman was once a slave. One night, she crept away from her Maryland **plantation** and walked to Pennsylvania where slavery was not allowed. People hid her along the way. She remembered the **route.** Over the next 10 years, she returned to the **South** 18 times and helped 300 slaves escape to freedom.

Slave owners wanted to stop Harriet Tubman. Some offered a $12,000 reward to anyone who caught her. No one ever did.

Parents did not tell their children about the plans to run away. Parents were afraid that the children might repeat the secret in front of the owner's family. So, on a quiet night, the parents woke the children and told them to get dressed. The next several weeks would be spent running and hiding.

On the **plantation,** slave children lived with their parents until the owner decided to sell them. If they reached the **North,** they usually could stay with their parents without fear.

Many children in the North never heard about slavery. But those whose parents were part of the Underground Railroad probably knew. During the night, there would be a knock at the door. The parents would ask, "Who's there?" The answer was, "I'm a friend with a friend." That was a signal that slaves needed to hide at the house.

If slaves were hiding in the house, the parents gave them food, water, and bandages if they needed them.

Hiding Places

Runaway slaves hid in forests—with snakes and wild animals! They hid in swamps with alligators and bugs!
If they were lucky, they finally reached a "station." Some people put flags or **lanterns** outside their houses. Some painted their chimneys with a row of white bricks. These were signals. Slaves had been told or learned that these houses were safe for hiding.

Today you can still see some houses that were part of the Underground Railroad. This house still stands in New York City.

These slaves quietly watch from their hiding place in a barn. **Slave catchers** are searching for runaway slaves. They will get a reward for returning slaves to their owners.

Slaves hid in the attics, in closets, in barns. Some houses had secret hiding places under the floor or behind a bookcase. Often the slaves left in a few hours. Sometimes they stayed awhile and worked to earn money or to recover from an injury.

21

Food

Runaway slaves had little time to eat. They were thankful for the food from the helpers on the Underground Railroad. In the woods, the slaves picked berries, apples, and nuts. Sometimes they caught a fish, or found a chicken. It was dangerous to build a cooking fire. A **slave catcher** might see the smoke.

ON THE GO
Runaway slaves
• drank water from streams and lakes
• caught fish, frogs, and toads with their bare hands.

These runaway slaves are resting and eating in a "station." They eat hoe-cakes — a type of biscuit made of cornmeal—and clabber, which is curdled sour milk.

Slave Recipe—Southern Biscuits

When slaves left the **plantation,** they could not carry much with them. They brought a few biscuits in their pockets so they would not get too hungry too soon. Below is a recipe for biscuits made by slaves in the **South.**

WARNING: Do not cook anything unless there is an adult to help you. Always ask an adult to remove food from a hot oven.

YOU WILL NEED
2 1/2 cups (600g) flour
1/4 cup (60 g) sugar
1 1/2 tablespoons
   baking powder
1/4 teaspoon salt
1/2 cup (120 g) butter
1 cup (240 ml) milk,
   or less
small amount of
vegetable oil

FOLLOW THE STEPS

1. Preheat the oven to 350 degrees Fahrenheit (180 Centigrade).
2. In a large bowl, mix together the flour, sugar, baking powder, and salt.
3. Use a fork to mash the butter into the mixture until it looks like coarse flour.
4. Slowly stir in the milk. Stop pouring the milk when the mixture is moist.
5. Rub a small amount of vegetable oil in a muffin tin. Then use a tablespoon to pour all the mixture in the muffin tin.
6. Bake in the oven until golden brown, about 35 minutes.
7. The recipe makes 12 biscuits.

Catching Slaves

Slave owners were furious about the Underground Railroad. They had bought their slaves with hard-earned money. They thought that anyone who helped slaves escape was a thief. Slave owners paid **slave catchers** to track down and return their slaves. Slave catchers hid in railroad stations and boat docks watching for slaves. They tramped through forests with **bloodhound** dogs.

These two slaves had escaped north to Boston, Massachusetts. The police caught them and returned them, by boat, to their angry owners in South Carolina.

In 1850, the U.S. **Congress** passed a new law. It said that slave catchers could look for slaves in the **North.** If they caught slaves, they could take them back to their owners in the **South.** Runaway slaves did not feel safe in the North after that. Many ran out of the country to Canada.

Some slave catchers caught any African Americans they saw. They caught people who had never been slaves. This poster warns everyone to beware of the slave catchers.

CAUTION !!
COLORED PEOPLE
OF BOSTON, ONE & ALL,

You are hereby respectfully CAUTIONED and advised, to avoid conversing with the

Watchmen and Police Officers of Boston,

For since the recent ORDER OF THE MAYOR & ALDERMEN, they are empowered to act as

KIDNAPPERS
AND
Slave Catchers,

And they have already been actually employed in KIDNAPPING, CATCHING, AND KEEPING SLAVES. Therefore, if you value your LIBERTY, and the *Welfare of the Fugitives* among you, *Shun* them in every possible manner, as so many *HOUNDS* on the track of the most unfortunate of your race.

Keep a Sharp Look Out for KIDNAPPERS, and have TOP EYE open.

APRIL 24, 1851.

On the Move

Some runaway slaves hid in carriages, trains, and steamboats. They tried to hide under the floors and behind boxes. The hidden slaves listened for the sounds of **slave catchers.** At a moment's notice, the slaves would have to jump off the train or boat and run away.

Often a river separated a **slave state** from a **free state.** Some slaves swam across the river or paddled on a raft made of logs. Others looked for a bridge to walk across.

Some slaves were lucky enough to ride on a steamboat along the Mississippi River. Then the trip north took just a few days.

Many runaway slaves walked all the way to freedom. It could take a year to reach a free state or Canada. They hurried through the night from one "station" to the next. The safe houses were about 10 to 20 miles (16 to 32 kilometers) apart. Bad weather, illness, and news about nearby slave catchers forced a change of **route** or slowed down the journey.

WINTER RIVERS

Many slaves decided to leave in the wintertime. The rivers were frozen and people could walk across.

Clothes for Hiding

Sometimes runaway slaves traveled in the passenger seats of trains and fancy steamboats. They would surely be noticed if they wore their ragged clothes from the **plantation.** So "conductors" gave the slaves dresses, suits, eyeglasses, hats, and wigs. Sometimes men dressed up as women and women dressed up as men.

When white "conductors" traveled with runaway slaves, the helpers pretended to own the slaves. It was not unusual for slaves to travel with their owners. But sometimes they ran into trouble.

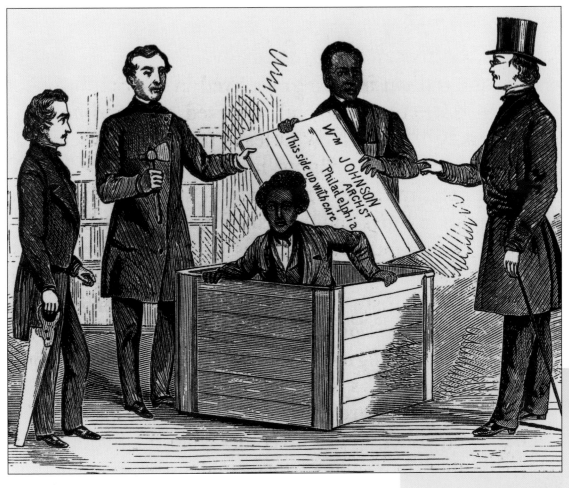

A slave named Henry Brown escaped from his plantation in a box. Someone built him a box and packed him inside with water, biscuits, and a tool to make air-holes. The box traveled on a train, a boat, and a wagon. A day later, Mr. Brown arrived at an **antislavery** office in Philadelphia. He was free.

As the story goes, Henry Brown's box was flipped upside down for 20 miles (32 km) of his journey. When the box was opened, his first words were, "How do you do, gentlemen?"

Freedom

When slaves reached a northern city, they began a new life. Many of them took jobs. They learned to read and write. Some of them changed their names because slaves often had their owners' last names.

The **North** and **South** argued about slavery for many years. They even fought a war over it. Finally in 1865, all the slaves were freed.

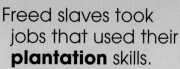

JOBS IN THE NORTH

Freed slaves took jobs that used their **plantation** skills.
- farm workers
- factory workers
- workers on fishing boats and railroads
- maids in houses and hotels
- nurses and babysitters

Some started small businesses.

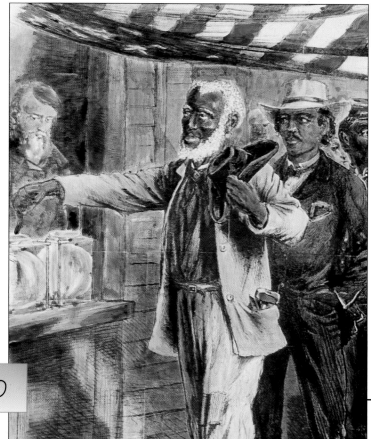

By 1870, African American men were allowed to vote, as shown here. Many white people in the South were not happy about this. They passed laws to stop African Americans from being treated as equals.

Glossary

antislavery against slavery

blacksmith person who makes things from iron

bloodhound large dog with a very good sense of smell

Congress part of the United States government that makes laws

crop plant grown to provide food or products to sell

free states in the United States, states that did not allow people to own slaves

lantern light with a frame around it. Before electricity, lanterns held candles or oil.

Native Americans first people living in the North American continent, also called American Indians

North in the United States, the states north of Maryland, the Ohio River, and Missouri; also called "free states," where slavery was not allowed

plantation large farm on which one main crop is grown, for example cotton

preacher someone who leads church services and gives a sermon

route the road or path to follow to get from one place to another

scent smell or odor of something or someone

slave catcher person who earns money by hunting and catching runaway slaves

slave states in the United States, states that allowed slavery

South in the United States, the states south of Pennsylvania and the Ohio River; also called "slave states"

More Books to Read

Ferris, Jeri. *Go Free or Die: A Story About Harriet Tubman.*
    Minneapolis, Minn.: Lerner Publishing Group, 1988.
Winter, Jeanette. *Follow the Drinking Gourd.*
    New York : Knopf, 1988.

Index